THE DREAMER

Dorian Petersen Potter

THE DREAMER

I want to dedicate this book of poetry to God,
my Lord and my Savior. He's always been in my life
the biggest and greatest inspiration of all.
Thank You Lord for all You had
done, and for your most wonderful gift of
love, forgiveness and salvation.

IN HIS LIGHT

(Senryu Suit)

His light is just great
Let it live within your heart
His light always glow

Walk in His perfect light
His light is divine
With Him you'll be fine

He forgives us all
All His blessings are around
Only pray to God

God is everywhere
His love lives right in my heart
Inspires my poetry

In His light I walk
Seek His guidance everyday
God help us through all.

*
****
*
*
*

~Learning~
(Egg Timer)

Learning is great fun
Just learn each day
Something new
You can
Yes
Yes
You can
Something new
Just learn each day
Learning is great fun

Right under the sun
In the moonlight
You can have
New goals
Dreams
Dreams
New goals
You can have
In the moonlight
Right under the sun.

*

*

~THE FALL SEASON~

(CHILD FOUR)

FALL
IT'S APPROACHING US SO FAST BY NOW
SOME OF HER SIGNS YOU CAN
JUST TELL

FALL
IT'S MAKING HER PRECIOUS PRESENCE KNOWN
TO YOU AND ME AND ALL
AROUND

FALL
IT'S A BEAUTIFUL SEASON WHEN THE
LEAVES CHANGE COLOURS AND AIR
GETS COOL.

*

*

~MOTHER NATURE~

(HAIKU)

JUST SAVE OUR PLANET

MOTHER NATURE IS CRYING

PLEADING WE HELP HER

*

~HIS LOVE~

(NONET)

I SEE GOD'S LOVE IN ALL THAT IS GOOD
COME WITH JOY AND JUST PRAISE HIS NAME
HE SHOWS HIS LOVE EVERYDAY
SEE HIS SMILE IN EACH ROSE
FORGIVES ALL OUR SINS
AND IN EACH CHILD
I CAN SEE
ALL HIS
LOVE

~THE CLOWN PIG~

(LIMERICK)

A WEIRD PIG OF A CERTAIN RENOWN

ONCE LIVED IN A HOUSE THAT WAS BROWN

BUT HE JUST DIDN'T CARE

FOR THERE CAME A BIG BEAR

WHO WEARING A GOWN MADE HIM A CLOWN!

~A BIG BIRD FROM CANTOON~

(LIMERICK)

A BIG BIRD FROM CANTOON COULD NOT FLY

WITH HIS WINGS SPREAD OPEN HE PERCH'D HIGH

BUT THE BRANCH THEN JUST BROKE

FELL AND IT WASN'T A JOKE

THOUGHT THAT HE WAS DEAD AND START'D TO CRY.

~ A LADY FROM NORTH WALES~

(LIMERICK)

A SILLY OLD LADY FROM NORTH WALES

ONE DAY DECIDED TO LOWER SALES

SO SHE JUST WENT TO TOWN

MARK'D ALL THE ITEMS DOWN

AND SURE ENOUGH SHE END'D UP IN JAIL!

~THE TOURIST~

(LIMERICK)

A FLORIDA TOURIST WITH CAMERA

SHOT MANY A ROLL FROM THE SIERRA

THEN JUST WENT TO HIS BED

BUT IN HIS HEAD WAS DREAD

WOKE UP SCAR'D RIGHT BESIDE HIM LAID HERA.

~HOPE~

(DOUBLE TETRACTYS)

HOPE
MAKES US
VERY STRONG
IT HELPS US DREAM
WHEN WE KEEP OUR HOPES THE SUN SHINES BRIGHTER

WITHOUT HOPE THE SUN DOESN'T SHINE,THERE'S NOTHING
YOU LOSE YOUR DREAMS
SO ALWAYS
KEEP YOUR
HOPES

*

*

~APPLES~

(NONET)

APPLES ARE VERY DELICIOUS FRUIT
SOME ARE RED YELLOW GOLD OR GREEN
THEY ALL TASTE SO VERY GOOD
"EAT AN APPLE A DAY
KEEP DOCTOR AWAY"
SOME FOLKS JUST SAY
APPLES ARE
GREAT FOR
YOU!

~THE NONET FORM~

(NONET)

THE NONET FORM IS DONE WITH NINE LINES.
COUNTING SYLLABLES FROM START TO END
THIS ONE HERE IS LINE SEVEN
NEXT GO WRITE LINE SIX AND
THEN DO LINES FIVE, FOUR

THREE,TWO, AND ONE
PERFECTLY
WRITTEN
DONE!

~GOD IS A LOVING GOD~

(DOUBLE TANKA)

GODS A LOVING GOD
NEVER LOSE YOUR FAITH IN HIM
HE'S ALWAYS WITH YOU
DO NOT LOSE FOCUS THROUGH LIFE
ISN'T EASY BUT KEEP FAITH

KEEP YOUR TRUST IN GOD
DON'T DOUBT THAT GOD WILL HELP YOU
GODS A LOVING GOD
HE'LL COME TO RESCUE EACH TIME
SMILE 'CAUSE WITH GOD WE CAN'T LOSE.

*

*

~NIGHT~
(PLEIADES)

NIGHT IT'S WONDERFUL TIME.
NICE TO REST AND RELAX.
NATURALLY DAYS DONE.
NEEDED TIME TO GET SOME SLEEP.
NEATH THE TREES THE MOON SHOWS.
NEAR YOU AND ME GOD LIVES.
NEW DAY ALWAYS BRINGS HOPES.

~WORDS~
(PLEIADES)

WORDS BEAUTIFULLY WRITTEN

WONDER WITH PAPER AND PEN
WANDERING EACH DAY HERE AND THERE
WADING INSIDE BRAIN EACH DAY
WALKING ALL THRU HAND IN HAND
WAITING FOR MUSE ALL THE TIME
WHILE PLAYING WITH WORDS AND FORMS.

*

~HAUNTINGS~

(CINQUAIN)

HAUNTINGS
TONIGHT TAKE TURN
MIDNIGHT MADNESS,SCREAMS SCREECH'S
THRU YOUR VEINS PASSES A CHILL,SO COLD
SO SCARY.

~HALLOWEEN NIGHT~

(DOUBLE WHITNEY)

HALLOWEEN
CELEBRATION
WHAT A NIGHT
CHILDREN HAVE FUN
DON COSTUMES
GO TRICK OR TREAT
CAN SEE WITCHES GHOULS AND GHOSTS

TONIGHT IS
HALLOWEEN
NIGHT OF FUN
IT'S SO CREEPY TOO
SO PEOPLE.

~THE BIBLE~

(FREUD)

THE BIBLE
SUCH GREAT BOOK
IT'S AMAZING!

MAKE SOME TIME
READ DAILY
SOW GOOD SEED

THROUGH ITS PAGES
FIND WISDOM
BEST TIME SPENT

INSTRUCTIONS
BEFORE WE
LEAVE THIS EARTH

GOD'S TEACHINGS
PAVE YOUR WAY
IN HEART STAY

THE BIBLE
TO FOLLOW
READ EACH DAY

IT HAS 66
BOOKS IN ALL
GREATEST BOOK!

~FALL~

(PLEIADES)

FALL IT'S WHEN LEAVES CHANGE,FALL.
FAVORITE TIME OF ALL.
FAIR WEATHER STAYS AWHILE.
FANTASTIC SIGHTS IN GREAT STYLE.
FANFARE OF COLORS 'ROUND.
FINE SEASON FULL OF SOUNDS.
FUN TIME FOR ALL ABOUNDS.

~A MESSAGE OF HOPE~

(MIXED AQUARIAN)

THE SUN
APPEARS
IT SHINES TODAY
SMILING THRU CLOUDS
IT'S FULL OF FUN AND WARMTH
GIVES MESSAGE OF HOPE TO
ME AND
YOU TOO.

~A FAT CAT~

(LIMERICK)

THERE ONCE WAS A VERY FAT CAT

WHO DIDN'T RECOGNIZE MOUSE FROM A GNAT

HE GOT ON TOP OF TABLE

BUT WAS NOT JUST ABLE

TO CATCH IT RIGHT FROM WHERE HE JUST SAT.

~A MAN FROM ONTARIO~

(SLIMERICK)

A MAN FROM ONTARIO CAME

ON ROCK STOOD-WANT'D FAME

HE SHOUT'D "LOOK AT ME!"

FLYING CAME A BEE

GOT STUNG

ON TONGUE

NOW HE'S ON HIS KNEE!

~TOTO THE CLOWN~

(TRIEL)

TOTO THE
CLUNKY CLOWN COULDNT STEP DOWN
HE LAUGHED,SANG SONGS WHICH SOUNDED ALL WRONG
THEN, OH NO! HIS PANTS DID FALL,SUSPENDERS NOT STRONG.

PANT WENT DOWN
FOLKS JUST LAUGHED,SOME DID YELL
TOTO THE CLOWN RAN BUT SLID ON HIS SKATE,
FOLKS AMAZED,WHEN TOTO THE CLOWN,FLEW AND FELL ON A PLATE!

*

~TOO SHORT AS IT IS~

(QUATERN)

LIFE IS JUST TOO SHORT AS IT IS
WE ALL NEED SOMEONE TO LOVE TO
YOU NEED TO THINK OF OTHERS TOO
DON'T THINK ALL THE TIME OF JUST YOU

THINK OF OTHERS WHO HAVE NEEDS TOO
LIFE IS JUST TOO SHORT AS IT IS
SOME GO THRU WORSE THINGS THAN WE DO
SO HELP,PRAY FOR THOSE THAT YOU KNOW

SOMETIMES WE HAVE TO TAKE A STAND
BE STRONG AND VOICE YOUR CONCERNS TOO
LIFE IS JUST TOO SHORT AS IT IS

SO BE TRUE AND BELIEVE IN YOU!

BELIEVE IN BETTER TOMORROW
DIRECT EMOTIONS TO CALMNESS
LIVE LIFE,LOVE LONG, ENJOY IT ALL
LIFE IS JUST TOO SHORT AS IT IS.

~I LOVE YOU~

(TRINE)

MY HEART BEATS FOR YOU
EVERY TIME I THINK OF YOU TO

YOU PUT IN MY HEART A SONG
AND MAKE ME ALL DAY STRONG

WHEN I THINK OF YOU I'M HAPPY
YOU TAKE ALL MY BLUES AWAY

I KNOW MY LOVE FOR YOU IS TRUE
WITH YOU I WANT TO SPEND WHOLE DAY LONG
I'M SO BLESS'ED YOU'RE IN MY LIFE EACH DAY.

*

~SUMMER 2011~

(DORIAN 42)

SUMMER IS FUN,SEASONS HOT
UMM, TEMPERATURE JUST SOAR!
MOVING 'ROUND, IS KIND OF HARD
MAKES ONE TIRED AND RAINS SOME MORE
END OF SUMMER BRINGS NEXT FALL
RAYS FROM SUN MOST FOLKS ADORE.

*

*

~DON'T KNOW WHAT LIES AHEAD~

(MONCHIELLE)

DON'T KNOW WHAT LIES AHEAD
WHAT WILL HAPPEN TOMORROW
SO EACH DAY JUST ENJOY
THANK GOD FOR ALL YOU HAVE
AND SHOUT HIS NAME WITH JOY

DON'T KNOW WHAT LIES AHEAD
LIVE EACH DAY LIKE IT'S LAST
PRAY FOR LOVED ONES EACH DAY
SHOW APPRECIATION
SEEK GOD IN ALL YOU DO

DON'T KNOW WHAT LIES AHEAD
BUT WITH GOD,DON'T WORRY MUCH
GOD KNOWS IT ALL,SEES HEART
HE FORGIVES,GIVES SALVATION
AND LOVES US ALL FROM START

DON'T KNOW WHAT LIES AHEAD
BUT GOD DOES,THATS ALL CARE
HE TELLS US HOW TO COPE
TRUST HIM,HE KNOWS BETTER
HE'S MY LIGHT,GIVES ME HOPE

*

~BECAUSE OF HIS LOVE~

(CONCRETE POEM)

BECAUSE
OF HIS
PURE LOVE
AND GRACE
I'M FREE AND SAVED TODAY
HE PAID THE UTMOST PRICE
WHEN CHOSE TO DIE FOR ME
AND YOU
HE DIED
FOR ALL
HE WAS
THE LAMB
AND TOOK

OUR PLACE
TO GIVE US LIFE.

*

~ALWAYS~

(QUATERN)

ALWAYS KEEP HOPE AND FAITH ALIVE
DON'T GIVE UP DREAMS BUT TRUST IN GOD
HE'S THE LIGHT THAT NEVER GOES OUT
LEARN HIS WAYS AND WALK IN HIS LIGHT

NO MATTER WHAT BELIEVE IN YOU
ALWAYS KEEP HOPE AND FAITH ALIVE
START BY MAKING SOME CHANGES TODAY
CONNECT TO GOD AND YOU'LL BE FINE

THINK POSITIVE THOUGHTS,REJECT BAD
LAUGHTERS GOOD FOR YOUR SOUL EACH DAY

ALWAYS KEEP HOPE AND FAITH ALIVE
NO MATTER WHAT BELIEVE IN YOU

DON'T STOP DREAMING,FOR DREAMS COME TRUE
YOU CAN MAKE YOUR DAY HAPPY,SAD
DO YOUR BEST IN ALL THAT YOU DO
ALWAYS KEEP HOPE AND FAITH ALIVE.

*

~CHAOS~

(RONDELET)

NOW IS CHAOS.
NOTHING BAD LIKE THIS ALL THESE YEARS.
NOW IS CHAOS.
SOUL HOLDS TO GODS SHINING BRIGHT LIGHT.
HE STANDS NEARS US, HE'S NEVER FAR.
NO MATTER WHERE ME OR YOU ARE.
NOW IS CHAOS.

~CHANGES~

(WHITNEY)

LET IT GO
GO WITH THE FLOW
CHANGES HAPPEN
YOU CAN'T STOP IT
THATS A FACT

SO WHEN CHANGES COME
RELAX AND JUST GO WITH IT.

*

~MY PRAYER TO YOU LORD~

(NOVE OTTO)

LORD GIVE ME YOUR STRENGTH AND HELP ME
'CAUSE THE BEST YOU WANT ME TO BE
CUP IN MY HEART YOU ALWAYS FILL
JUST CLEAN MY HEART AND SOUL YOUR WAY.
TAKE AWFUL DEPRESSION AWAY
HELP ACT ACCORDING TO YOUR WILL

YOU'RE WITH ME AND THATS ALL I KNOW
YOU PROTECT AND HELP ME TO GROW
AND YOU HEAL MY SOUL WHEN FALLS ILL.

~DON'T WASTE YOUR DAY~

(TANKA)

DO NOT WASTE YOUR DAY
JUST MAKE ALL YOUR DREAMS COME TRUE
THERE'S NO TIME TO LOSE
DREAM AND TRY NOT TO LOOK BACK
LIVE DAY AS IF WAS LAST

*

~LORD HEAR MY PRAYERS~

(MONOTETRA)

LORD HEAR MY PRAYERS,COME HELP ME
"CAUSE THE BEST YOU WANT ME TO BE
YOU KNOW PROBLEMS,ALL YOU CAN SEE

FROM EVIL I FLEE.FROM EVIL I FLEE.

CLEAN HEART AND SOUL, DO IT YOUR WAY
I CAN DO ANYTHING WITH YOU
ANYTHING THAT'S RIGHT AND NEED TO
LORD BLESS MY DAY.LORD BLESS MY DAY.

YOU'RE WITH ME AND THATS ALL I KNOW
HERE IN MY HEART YOU'RE HAPPY SONG
YOU ALWAYS HELP AND WITH YOU GROW
MY SPIRIT GLOW.MY SPIRIT GLOW.

*

~SUMMER SHOWERS~

(STYLE NO-ONES)

TODAY
SO HOT AGAIN
TEMPERATURE IS RISING MORE

AND SHOWERS FALL
EACH DAY

THEN AFTER
STORM OR RAIN IT GETS WORSE
HEAT AND HUMIDITY REACHES ITS HEIGHT
IT IS SUFFOCATING
HARD TO BREATHE

HEAT IS JUST TOO MUCH
RIGHT HERE IN SOUTH FLORIDA SO EXTREME
RAIN REFRESHES FOR AWHILE

*

~PRAYERS ARE PRIVATE CONVERSATIONS~

(TANKA)

PRAYERS ARE PRIVATE
CHATS JUST BETWEEN YOU AND GOD

YOU CAN GO TO HIM
FOR ANYTHING YOU NEED AND
GOD ANSWERS ACCORDINGLY.

~QUIET MIND~

(DOUBLE WHITNEY)

QUIET MIND
LOTS TAKING PLACE
I CAN'T GRASP

GOD,NONE IS RIGHT
QUIET MIND GIVE ME YOUR PEACE.

CAN'T STOP THIS
GIVE ALL TO YOU
IN YOUR HANDS

YOU KNOW WHATS BEST
YOUR WILL BE DONE I TRUST YOU!

~COME WITH ME TODAY~

(EIGHT BY FOUR)

COME WITH ME MY
FRIEND,LET'S ENJOY
THIS HANDSOME DAY.
LOOK AT THE SUN
IT'S SHINING NOW
LET'S HAVE CUP OF
COFFEE, TEA, EAT
WHILE WE TALK,LAUGH.

AS WE DO THIS
LET'S PRAY TO GOD
FOR ALL OUR DEAR
FAMILY AND
FRIENDS, AND JUST
FOR EVERYONE
COME, SIT WITH ME
LET'S ENJOY DAY!

~REMEMBER~

(TRIOLET)

YOU'RE A SPECIAL PERSON ONE OF A KIND
AND A CHILD OF THE MASTER,HE MADE YOU
WALK IN HIS LIGHT AND HIS GRACE YOU'LL FIND
YOU'RE A SPECIAL PERSON ONE OF A KIND
REMEMBER HE LOVES YOU, KEEP THAT IN MIND
HE WATCHES YOUR BACK, PROTECT YOU FROM THE FOE
YOU'RE A SPECIAL PERSON ONE OF A KIND
AND A CHILD OF THE MASTER, HE MADE YOU.

~HOT~

(TRIOLET)

TODAY IS A VERY HOT DAY
HUMIDITY MAKING ME MAD
HAD RAINED A LOT BUT NOW SUNS HIGH
TODAY IS A VERY HOT DAY
GLAD TO KNOW THIS WEATHER WON'T STAY
TEMPERATURES SOARING,THATS BAD!
TODAY IS A VERY HOT DAY
HUMIDITY MAKING ME MAD.

*

~LIFE IS BEAUTIFUL~

(TRINET)

START THE
DAY HAPPY
WITH A SMILE AND GOOD ATTITUDE
FIRST THING,SPEND TIME WITH GOD
PRAY,SHOW
FAMILY,FRIENDS
YOU CARE.

SEEK GOD
IN ALL
THAT YOU DO ALL THE TIME
BE POSITIVE AND SMILE EACH DAY
PRAISE GOD
THANK HIM
FOR EVERYTHING.

REMEMBER THAT
EACH DAY
IS REALLY A BLESSING FROM HIM
LIFE IS BEAUTIFUL NO MATTER WHAT
THANK GOD
FOR ALL
YOU HAVE.

*

~HE HAS MANY NAMES~

(TRINET)

JESUS' NAME
MEANS "SAVIOUR"
JESUS HAS LONG LIST OF NAMES
THE BIBLE SAYS THAT, IT'S TRUE
EMMANUEL, CHRIST,
RABBI, SON
OF GOD.

SON OF
DAVID, SON
OF MAN, AND PRINCE OF PEACE,
LAMB OF GOD, THE ANNOINTED ONE,
THE WORD,
I AM,
AND MORE.

LORD OF
LORDS, ALPHA
AND OMEGA AND KING OF KINGS,
BRIGHT MORNING STAR, LION OF JUDAH,
ALL JESUS
NAMES. I
BELIEVE IT.

*

~ANYDAY ~

(UNMETERED RHYMING COUPLETS)

DON'T PUSH AWAY OR KILL ANY OF YOUR DREAMS TODAY OR ANYDAY.
LIFE'S TOO SHORT SO DONT WASTE IT AND THROW IT ALL AWAY.
LISTEN TO THE RHYTHMS AND THE MUSIC INSIDE YOUR HEART.
THERE'LL BE MUSIC TILL THINGS MAY START TO FALL FOR YOU APART.
TODAY IT MAY BE ME BUT TOMORROW IT MAY BE ALSO THEM OR YOU.
CRUEL WORDS CAN REALLY HURT AND MAKE US ALL SOMETIMES OH SO BLUE.
FEELINGS AND EMOTIONS ARE NOT SOME THAT ONE DAY IN YOU OR ME JUST GREW.
THEY HAVE BEEN THERE AS PART OF YOU AND ME ALWAYS WILL BE THEY'RE NOT NEW.
WITH FAITH AND STRENGH WE CAN ADVANCE FORTH AND MAKE WITH WORK OUR LITTLE WAY.
DURING YOUR JOURNEY YOU'LL FALL SOMETIMES BUT HAVE TO GET UP AND WALK TALL TOO.
PEOPLE,LIFE AND THINGS ARE NOT LIKE THEY MAY SEEM SOMETIMES ALWAYS TO BE.
YOU CAN DO IT ALL,EVERYTHING IT IS POSSIBLE,IF YOU ONLY DARE TO DREAM IT AND SEE.

~CELEBRATE LIFE~

(DEE'S FIVE-SEVEN-TEN)

LET'S CELEBRATE LIFE
PUSH BACK ALL THE STRIFE
WATCH THE CLOCK TICKING BY FAST
DON'T THROW LIFE AWAY
CAST YOUR CARES TODAY
GIVE THEM TO GOD, HIS JOY LAST

THANK THE LORD RIGHT NOW
TIME WON'T WAIT THAT'S HOW
THANK HIM FOR ALL THAT YOU HAVE
ENJOY LIFE, HAVE HOPE
WITH GOD YOU CAN COPE
THRU HIS SON ALL HE CAN SAVE

GOODNESS IN HIM FIND
OPEN YOUR HEART, MIND
THERE'S STILL LOVE, LISTEN TO HEART
SEE LIGHT, DON'T BE BLIND
SHOW YOU CARE AND MIND
DON'T LET FOLKS RIP HEART APART

CELEBRATE LIFE OPEN YOUR HEART WIDE
REGAIN LOST DREAMS, CLIMB MOUNTAIN
REACH OUT TO GOD AND TOUCH EACH SOUL YOU CAN
PRAY GOD FOR ALL MEN'S SINS, STAINS.

~HIS WONDROUS LOVE~

(FREE STYLE)

LOVE IS ALL THAT HE TEACHES US
SINCE THE DAY HE WAS BORN,
THAT TOOK PLACE TWO-
THOUSAND
YEARS AGO THIS MORN.

HIS WONDROUS LOVE
TRANSCENDS ALL WE KNOW,
FROM CHILD TO GROWN ADULT
WITH ALL MY LOVE TO HIM I BOW.

THERE'S NOTHING IN THE WORLD
HE COULDN'T DO FOR YOU;
HE KNOWS ALL YOUR NEEDS
AND WHAT'S BEST FOR YOU TOO.

HE LEFT US THE HOLY BIBLE TO READ,
AND SPREAD IT ALL OVER THE WORLD, AS HE SAID.

*

~MORE VALUABLE THAN GOLD~

(FREE STYLE)

THERE ARE TIMES WHEN THIS LIFE
CAN REALLY WEIGHT US ALL DOWN,
MOMENTS OF HAPPINESS ARE JUST A FEW AND;
IF YOU ASK ME THERE ARE NOT MANY OF THOSE AROUND.

LIFE MOST OF THE TIME IS LIKE A "MERRY GO 'ROUND,
IT'S LIKE A CIRCUS AND ALL OF US ARE LIKE THE "DRAMA CLOWN,"
WE NEED TO BE CAREFUL OF WHERE AND HOW WE WALK,
AND ALSO NEED TO BE WEARY OF THE WAY THAT WE TALK.

THERE ARE SO MANY GREAT THINGS IN LIFE THAT WE CAN DO,
SOMETIMES LITTLE THINGS WE DO ARE MORE IMPORTANT THAN BIG ONE;
AT TIMES WE TEND TO FORGET HOW TO REALLY BOND TOGETHER,
WITH FAMILY AND FRIENDS, AND THEY'RE SUCH A GREAT PART OF YOU.

LIFE IS TOO PRECIOUS AND SHORT TO WASTE IT, AND THAT YOU WELL KNOW,
AND FAMILY AND FRIENDS ARE MORE VALUABLE TO ME THAN PURE GOLD, AND THATS SO.

~AMONG FRIENDS~

(FUNNY TANKA/SENRYU)

TWO WOMEN TALKING
ABOUT THE NEW HUNK IN THE
HOOD."BUT HE ACTS SO
STUPID,"SAID FRIEND TO OTHER
"I THINK HE MUST HAVE HIS BRAIN,

RIGHT BETWEEN HIS LEGS."
"YEAH," HER FRIEND SIGHED,"BUT I'D STILL
SURELY LOVE TO BLOW HIS MIND."

~TIME IS VERY IMPORTANT~

(TANKA)

TIME IS IMPORTANT
TIME FLIES AND CAN NOT BE STOPPED
IT GOES BY TOO FAST
TIME HANGS JUST HEAVILY SOMETIMES
WE LIVE LIFE SCHEDULE BY CLOCKS.

~TO WHAT IT COMES DOWN TO~

(A FUNNY TANKA POEM)

FIRST YEAR OF MARRIAGE,
MAN SPEAKS AND WOMAN LISTENS;
SECOND, WOMAN SPEAKS,
AND MAN LISTENS,THIRD YEAR BOTH
SPEAK AND THE NEIGHBORS LISTEN.

~FINE LIKE AGED WINE~

(A FUNNY TANKA POEM)

I TOLD MY WIFE THAT
A MAN IS LIKE FINE WINE,I
ALWAYS GET BETTER
WITH AGE.THE NEXT DAY SHE
LOCK'D ME IN THE WINE CELLAR!

*

~YOU'RE THE BEST THAT THERE IS~

(EIGHT BY FOUR)

YOU MEAN THE WORLD
TO ME AND MORE
WITHOUT YOU THERE'S
NO ONE FOR ME
YOU LOVE ME TRUE
GIVE ME THE BEST
YOU SEND ME SWEET
THOUGHTS ALL DAY LONG.

I'M SO HAPPY
YOU'RE IN MY LIFE
IN EVERYTHING
SKY ARE BLUER
BECAUSE OF YOU
AND YOUR TRUE LOVE
YOU GIVE ME FOR
ETERNITY.

~TRUST~

(MINUTE POETRY)

NO MATTER WHAT, ALWAYS TRUST GOD.
IT IS NOT ODD
HE HELPS ME GROW
PROTECTS MY SOUL.

ENJOY DAY, PRAY FOR TOMORROW.
SEND WOES AWAY!
SEEK THE SUNSHINE
LET YOUR HEART SHINE.

TAKE THINGS IN YOUR LIFE SOMETIME SLOW.
GO WITH THE FLOW
TRUST GOD EACH DAY.

*

~KITTENS 1~

(WHITNEY)

KITTENS CUTE
GO TO MOM CAT
SHE LICKS THEM

THEY TOO SHOW LOVE
AND PLAYFULLY BITE HER TAIL.

~KITTENS 2~

(WHITNEY)

SOFT AND SWEET
ADORABLE!
LOVED WATCH THEM

THET TOUCHED MY HEART
SO SAD THAT I COULDN'T KEEP THEM.

~OF NAILS AND WOOD~

(A FUNNY TANKA)

INNKEEPER: ROOMS $15
A NIGHT.IT'S $5 IF YOU MAKE
YOUR OWN BED.GUEST SAYS:
I'LL MAKE MY OWN.INKEEPER:
"GREAT," GET YOU SOME NAILS AND WOOD!

~TIME~

(MIRRORED TANKA)

THERE'S BARELY A TIME
AND IT'S FLOWING RIGHT THRU HANDS
CAN'T STOP OR GO BACK
TIME LIKE PRICELESS REFINED GOLD
INSIDE PROBING MIND UNFOLD
INSIDE PROBING MIND UNFOLD
TIME LIKE PRICELESS REFINED GOLD
CAN'T STOP OR GO BACK
AND IT'S FLOWING RIGHT THRU HANDS
THERE'S BARELY A TIME.

*

~IN HIS LIGHT~

(MODIFIED LUC BAT)

TRY TO WALK IN HIS LIGHT
SOULS TIRED WHEN COMES THE NIGHT AGAIN
WITH DREAMS BOUND IN THE NIGHT
ONLY WITH GOD, HEART MIGHT THEN SING
CAN'T GIVE UP NOW MY FIGHT
MY SPIRIT IN HIS LIGHT SHALL CLING
TRY TO WALK IN HIS LIGHT
ONLY WITH GOD,HEART MIGHT THEN SING.

~MOONLIGHT~

(MIRRORED TANKA)

MOON IN SKY SO BRIGHT
WITH HER HEART EMBRACES NIGHT
SHE DANCES IN THE LIGHT
HER GRACEFUL FACE SHOWS THRU CLOUDS
BARES IT ALL HIGH IN THE SKY
BARES IT ALL HIGH IN THE SKY
HER GRACEFUL FACE SHOWS THRU CLOUDS
SHE DANCES IN THE LIGHT
WITH HER HEART EMBRACES NIGHT
MOON IN SKY SO BRIGHT.

~I GIVE YOU MY LOVE~

(MIRRORED RONDELET)

GIVE YOU MY LOVE
SEE THE SKY WITH STARS AND THE MOON
GIVE YOU MY LOVE
SENT TO US ALL WAY FROM ABOVE
AS NIGHT LEAVES BRINGS PROMISING DAWN
GRACEFULLY LOVE GLIDES LIKE A SWAN
GIVE YOU MY LOVE
GIVE YOU MY LOVE
GRACEFULLY LOVE GLIDES LIKE A SWAN
AS NIGHT LEAVES BRINGS PROMISING DAWN
SENT TO US ALL WAY FROM ABOVE
GIVE YOU MY LOVE
SEE THE SKY WITH STARS AND THE MOON
GIVE YOU MY LOVE.

*

~LOVE IS NOT JUST A STATE OF MIND~

(BRACE OCTAVE)

LOVE IS A VERY BEAUTIFUL FEELING
CAN MAKE YOU SAPPY OR HAPPY
AND AT TIMES CAN GIVE YOU HEALING
SOMETIMES MAKES US SO UNHAPPY
YOU REACH THE STARS OR HIT THE CEILING
EMOTIONS MAKES US SAD OR HAPPY
LOVE IS NOT JUST A STATE OF MIND
FOR IN YOUR HEART LOVE YOU CAN FIND.

~I FOCUS MY EYES ON HIM EACH DAY~

(SPANISH HUITAIN)

FOCUS MY EYES ON HIM EACH DAY
HE'S ALWAYS WITH ME WHEN IN NEED
JESUS IS BEST FRIEND I DO SAY
HE DWELLS IN MY HEART AND HEAD
HIS WORDS INSPIRES ME WHEN READ
WITH ME WHENEVER I DO GO
HE'S ALWAYS THERE WHEN I'M IN NEED
BRINGS JOY WHEN PAIN IN MY HEART GROW.

~HELP ME GOD~

(JESUS TEARS)

OH
MY GOD
HELP ME NOW
HEARTS VERY SAD
I'M BROKEN IN HALF
TO YOU I COME
HELP THE BLIND
JUST SEE
NOW

I'M
DROWNING
IN DESPAIR
CAN'T COPE WITH THIS
WATERS DEEP
CAN'T KEEP AFLOAT
I'M SINKING
WITH HIM
NOW.

*

~CAUTION, CROSSROAD AHEAD~

(UNMETERED QUATRAIN)

JUST AHEAD THERE'S IS THIS CROSSROAD
FEELING LIKE TIMES BORROWED
WONDERFUL DREAMS YOU'RE JUST TOSSING
VOWS NO MORE HONOURING.

WE'VE BEEN TOGETHER ALL THIS TIME
NOW YOU QUIT WHAT A CRIME
YOU JUST WANT TO THROW ALL THIS 'WAY
AND HEARTS BREAKING EACH DAY.

WHY YOU'RE DOING THIS,TO ALL, ME
SPLITTING THIS FAMILY
WE TRY TO UNDERSTAND YOUR REASON
BUT STILL WRONG, IT'S TREASON.

SEE THAT LOVE ALONE CAN'T HOLD YOU
WHAT CAN I LONGER DO?
YOU'VE DECIDED ALL, REST, LEFT UNSAID
PRAY GOD, HEART LEADS YOUR HEAD.

*

~THE RED THE WHITE AND THE BLUE~

(FREE VERSE)

LET'S ALL STAND BY THE RED
THE WHITE AND THE BLUE,
THERE SHE STANDS IN ALL HER
GLORY
AND IN ALL HER COLORS SO
PROUD.

SHE MAY BE BURNT AND BY SOME
PEOPLE TORN APART
BUT THERE SHE STILL STANDS
VERY, VERY PROUD,
IN THE HOUSES, IN THE BUILDINGS
FLYING ALWAYS,
ALWAYS UNTOUCHED IN THE WIND.

AND IN THE HEARTS OF THE BRAVE
THE PROUD AND THE FREE,
SHE'S MUCH LOVED BY ME AND
ALL OF US
THAT BELIEVE IN HER CAUSE AND
HER DREAMS,
SO SHE WILL ALWAYS STAND IN
OUR HEARTS, NO MATTER WHAT,
IN ALL HER RADIANT COLORS OF
RED, WHITE AND BLUE....
FLYING HIGHER AND VERY PROUD
IN ALL THE HEARTS OF THE BRAVE
AND THE FREE,
AND ALL THE ONES THAT WE LOVE
AND DEFEND LIBERTY.

~IF I WAS A KID AGAIN~

(RHYMING UNMETERED QUATRAIN)

OH IF I WAS A KID AGAIN
I WOULD PLAY ALL OVER THE PLACE
RUN DOWN WITH MY PET DOG AND DOLL
THE ONE WITH PRETTY DRESS AND FACE

I'D LAUGH AND FLY SO HIGH MY KITE
PICK ONE WITH THE COLORS MORE BRIGHT
RED,YELLOWS,PURPLE,GREENS AND BLUE
PLAY OUTSIDE TILL ARRIVES THE NIGHT

IF I WAS A CHILD ONE MORE TIME
I'D MAKE SURE THAT I HAVE MORE FUN
PLAY WITH ALL MY FAVORITE TOYS
AND PLAY WITH MY FRIENDS TILL DAYS DONE.

*

~DOLLHOUSE~

(SONNETINA RISPETTO)

I JUST LOVE MY PRETTY DOLLHOUSE
IN IT KEEP MY DOLLS BUT NO MOUSE
MY DOLLS ARE SPECIAL TO ME
SOME ARE SO OLD BUT STILL ARE NICE

MANY COST DEAR HAVE HIGH TAG PRICE
CLOWN DOLLS MAKE ME SMILE AND GLEE
I JUST LOVE MY PRETTY DOLLHOUSE
IN IT KEEP MY DOLLS, BUT NO MOUSE

MY DOLLS ARE REALLY AMAZING
THEY'RE SO CUTE AND SMILES DO BRING
MY DOLLS ARE SPECIAL TO ME
SOME ARE SO OLD BUT STILL ARE NICE

I JUST LOVE MY PRETTY DOLLHOUSE
IN IT KEEP MY DOLLS, BUT NO MOUSE.

*

~SADNESS~

(SONNETINA RISPETTO)

SADNESS CAME TO VISIT TODAY
IT WASN'T EASY BUT SENT HER AWAY
AS SHE CAME TORTURED MY POOR SOUL
SHE GAVE ME HER COLD KISS OF DEATH

AS I COULD PUSHED HER ASIDE 'NEATH
SHE LEFT IN MY SOUL A BLACK HOLE
SADNESS CAME TO VISIT TODAY
IT WASN'T EASY BUT SENT HER AWAY

GOD'S SWEET VOICE THEN TALKED TO ME TOO
"HAVE NO FEAR, I'M STILL WITH YOU TO"
AS SHE CAME TORTURED MY POOR SOUL
SHE GAVE ME HER COLD KISS OF DEATH

SADNESS CAME TO VISIT TODAY
IT WASN'T EASY BUT SENT HER AWAY.

~HIS TESTS~

(MINUTE POETRY)

GOD TEST US YES ALL OF THE TIME
BUT WITH HIM CLIMB.
WITH FAITH AND HOPE
HE HELPS ME COPE.

FOR ME BELIEVING IS A MUST.
WON'T TURN TO DUST
KEEP ALL MY DREAMS
THOUGH SOMETIMES DEEM.

NEED STRENGHTEN SOUL EVERY SINGLE DAY
GOD HELPS ME THROUGH.
HE HOLDS ME UP
REFILLS MY CUP.

*

~MANGO TREE~

(MIRRORED TANKA)

MANGO FALLS FROM TREE
RIPE, DELICIOUS AND SO SWEET
MANGO TREE SO TALL
IT GIVES SUCH A TASTY FRUIT
MANGO DROPS NEAR TOP OF HEAD
MANGO DROPS NEAR TOP OF HEAD
IT GIVES SUCH A TASTY FRUIT
MANGO TREE SO TALL
RIPE, DELICIOUS AND SO SWEET
MANGO FALLS FROM TREE.

*

~BEAUTIFUL AND FREE~

(OCTELLE)

I'M THE RED, THE WHITE AND THE BLUE
STAND WITH HONOUR FOR ME AND YOU
CELEBRATE TODAY WITH ME
I'LL FLY AND WAVE TO THE SKY
TODAY IS FOURTH OF JULY
FOR FREEDOM PAID PRICE SO HIGH
I'M THE RED,THE WHITE AND THE BLUE
STAND WITH HONOUR FOR ME AND YOU.

*

~SUCCESS~

(DOUBLE TANKA)

ALWAYS DO YOUR BEST
WHATEVER TASK BIG OR SMALL
YOU CAN SUCCEED
SKY HAS NO LIMIT YOU KNOW
SOAR HIGH LET NOTHING STOP YOU

YOU CAN PASS EACH TEST
WITH FLYING COLORS DO IT
SET A GOAL TRY IT
ACHIEVE ALL YOU HAVE IN MIND
FINISH RACE JUST DO YOUR BEST.

~GRACE~

(DOUBLE TANKA)

IN YOU CAN SEE GRACE
YOU MAKE ME FEEL DIFFERENT
BRING ME ONLY GOOD
WITH YOU CAN FIND JUST BEAUTY
YOU ALWAYS FILL ME WITH PEACE

SPREAD RADIANT MERCY
HEAVENLY WONDERFUL GRACE
SEEK EACH DAY YOUR FACE
BRING DIVINE INSPIRATION
WITH YOU CAN SOAR SKY SO HIGH.

~POETRY~

(FREE STYLE)

I LIKE TO WRITE MY POETRY
AND I DO IT BECAUSE IT MAKES FEEL SO GOOD INSIDE WHEN I DO.
I FIND IT SO COMFORTING TO WRITE JUST FOR ME EVERYDAY;
AND I LOVE TO WRITE SOME OF MY POETRY FOR YOU TOO!

I LIKE TO WRITE MY POETRY
ALTHOUGH, IT GETS HARD AT TIMES, TO DO.
I ALSO ENJOY READING YOUR POETRY
I LOVE TO READ ABOUT WHAT YOU WRITE TOO.

I FIND THAT WRITING POETRY IS VERY GOOD FOR ME,
AND IT'S A GREAT THERAPY FOR ME AND YOU TOO!
IT CAN BE SUCH A GOOD EXERCISE FOR YOUR MIND,
IT CAN BESTOW YOU WITH GOOD FEELINGS, OF EVERY KIND.

I LOVE TO WRITE POETRY ABOUT YOU BUT NOT ME,
MY LIFE IS NOT THAT VERY INTERESTED YOU SEE,
BUT I FIND THAT YOURS THROUGH MY EYES IT IS,
MY LIFE IS COMPLETELY BORED, BUT I FIND THAT YOURS IT'S NOT.

I WRITE MY POETRY ALL THE TIME, TO PLEASE MYSELF FIRST,
I WORK HARD AT WHAT I DO TO MAKE IT BETTER AND NOT WORST.
TO IMPROVE IT I'VE WRITING IT LIKE FOREVER, EVERYDAY,
I CAN'T PLEASE EVERYBODY, SO I NEVER TRY TO PLEASE ANYONE.

BUT I'M PLEASED TO HEAR THAT SOME OF YOU ENJOY MY POETRY,
AND I WISH TO SEND A BIG "THANK YOU" TO ALL MY READERS TOO,
THANK YOU FOR READING SOME OF POETRY EVERYDAY,
THANKS FOR LEAVING ME YOUR FEEDBACK AND SIGNING MY GUESTBOOK
THE OTHER DAY.

I RATHER MAKE YOU SMILE AND LAUGH,
WHEN YOU CALL ON ME AND READ MY POETRY.
MOST OF THE TIME I JUST WRITE ABOUT YOU AND NOT ME,
AND I REALLY LOVE TO WRITE ABOUT EVERYTHING I SEE.

I RATHER MAKE YOU SMILE AND LAUGH,

THAN CRY WHEN YOU COME TO READ MY POETRY.
MUSIC OR NOT MUSIC, I LOVE WRITING MY POETRY EVERYDAY,
AND I LIKE IT JUST THE WAY IT IS, AND THIS WAY IT SHALL STAY.

I WOULD LIKE TO PLEASE EVERYBODY ALL THE TIME EVERYWHERE,
BUT THAT CAN NOT BE DONE BY ME OR ANYONE ANYWHERE.
BUT I AM SO PLEASED TO HEAR THAT YOU STILL LIKE MY POETRY,
AND I WANT TO SEND YOU A BIG THANK YOU TO YOU, MY READER TOO.

I WRITE MY POETRY ALL THE TIME, TO PLEASE, MYSELF FIRST,
I WORK HARD AT WHAT I DO TO MAKE IT BETTER AND NOT WORST.
I FIND IT SO COMFORTING TO WRITE JUST FOR ME EVERYDAY,
AND I LOVE TO WRITE SOME OF MY POETRY FOR YOU TOO!

*

~ANOTHER DAY AGAIN~

(PANTOUM)

ANOTHER DAY HAS FLOWN BY AGAIN TODAY
AND THEN THE NIGHT APPROACHES FAST
BRINGING TO ME SWEET DREAMS OF YOU
AS I WATCH THE MOON AND STARS AT LAST.

AND THEN THE NIGHT APPROACHES FAST
AND HERE IN MY HEART I ALWAYS HAVE YOU
AS I WATCH THE MOON AND STARS AT LAST
I JUST WISH YOU WERE HERE WITH ME TOO.

AND THEN THE NIGHT APPROACHES FAST
BRINGING SWEET DREAMS OF YOU TO ME
AS I WATCH THE MOON AND STARS AT LAST
YOUR FACE IS THE ONLY THING I SEE.

AND THEN THE NIGHT APPROACHES FAST
BRINGING TO ME SWEET DREAMS OF YOU
AS I WATCH THE MOON AND STARS AT LAST
ANOTHER DAY HAS FLOWN BY AGAIN TODAY.

*

~TO ALL MY DEAR FRIENDS~

(TRIPLE TANKA)

IN TIME OF TROUBLE
I'LL ALWAYS BE THERE FOR YOU
IF YOU WANT ME TO
YOU JUST HAVE TO ASK ME THAT
AND I'LL BE THERE FOR SURE TO.

MAY GOOD LORD KEEP YOU
ILLUMINATE EACH STEP YOU TAKE
MAY HE BE WITH YOU
AND KEEP YOU IN GOOD HEALTH
MAY SUN SHINE ON YOU EACH DAY.

YOU ARE BEAUTIFUL
IN EVERYTHING INSIDE,OUT
JUST REMEMBER THAT
LET NO ONE TELL YOU OTHERWISE
YOU'RE JUST SO SPECIAL TO ME!

*

~CONNECTING~

(DOUBLE TANKA)

CONNECTING IS GREAT
IT BRINGS PEOPLE TOGETHER
FOR GOOD CAUSE UNITE
STRENGTHENS TIES AND BRING SMILES
WITH FAMILY FRIENDS THEN START.

ONLINE FRIENDS ARE NICE
ADD A LINK, JOIN A CHALLENGE
BE PART OF SOME GREAT
MAKE IT HAPPEN AND HAVE FUN
COME ON FRIENDS CONNECT WITH ME.

*

~AN SMILE~

(TRIPLE SENRYU)

EVERYDAY JUST SMILE
REMEMBER LIFE IS TOO SHORT
SO TRY TO MAKE IT WORTHWHILE

AN SMILE IS SO NICE
CAN BRING SUNSHINE TO ANYONE
IT'S NOT HARD TO SMILE

EVEN HEART BE SAD
SMILING CAN OPEN A DOOR
AND SPREAD SUNSHINE IN HEARTS.

*

*

~SOUTHERN PLANTATIONS~

(DOUBLE TANKA)

MAGNIFICENT GREAT HOMES
FILL'D OF MUCH HISTORY AND BEAUTY
MAJESTIC JEWELS
FILL WITH MANY MEMORIES
SOME SO GOOD SOME SO BAD

SUN IS GOING DOWN
ANCIENT WALLS SHOW AMIDT OAK TREES
MANY STAND SO TALL
SURVIVING TIME MANY WARS
ELEGANT HOMES EXUDING SUCH GRACE.

*

~RAINBOWS~

(TRIPLE TANKA)

SHOWING IN THE SKY
DISPLAYING COLOURS SO BRIGHT
MAGNIFICENTLY
DECLARATION OF BEAUTY
GREAT PROMISE OF LOVE AND GRACE

AFTER ALL THE RAIN
ROADS AND STREETS WASHED CLEAN AGAIN
PEACEFUL AND SERENE
RADIANT RAINBOWS APPEAR
IN GLORIOUS NICE COLORS

A LOVING PROMISE
YOU GIVE US ALWAYS RAINBOWS
MOST BEAUTIFUL VIEWS
THANK YOU FOR HEAVENLY SIGHT
FOR HOPE AND LOVE YOU SHOW US.

~BELIEVE~

(TRIPLE SENRYU)

BELIEVE IN YOURSELF
NO MATTER WHAT OTHERS THINK
DO JUST WHAT IS RIGHT

EACH DAY DO YOUR BEST
EVERYDAY RENEW YOUR MIND
SET GOOD GOALS IN LIFE

DO ALWAYS SOME GOOD
TAKE GOOD CARE OF YOURSELF TOO
STRENGTHEN YOUR SPIRIT

*

~WITH HIS BLESSINGS~

(KEY TO MY HEART)

IT'S
VERY
HARD DAY
FOR ME
TODAY
COME TO********ME GOD
PRAY THAT YOU HELP ME ACCEPT SOME THINGS
PLEASE GIVE ME MORE STRENGTH AND WISDOM
WITH YOU I CAN NOT FALL
WITH YOU ENDURE IT ALL
IN YOUR WINGS CAN FLY
YOU PROTECT ME
FROM EVIL
GUIDE ME
THRU THIS
JOURNEY
YOU'RE WITH ME
NOW AND YOU
ALWAYS
WILL BE
TILL THE
END

About the Author

Dorian Petersen Potter has been writing poetry for most of her life. Her poetry has been published in many anthologies and poetry collections all over the world. Her poetry today can be found in many places in the internet and in several of her poetry pages too.

Dorian's personal websites:

"Poetic Dreams"

http://www.PoetryPoem.com/ladydp2000

and

http://publishing with passion.com/dorianpetersenpotter.html

www.ingramcontent.com/pod-product-compliance
Ingram Content Group UK Ltd.
Pitfield, Milton Keynes, MK11 3LW, UK
UKHW041918190726
13854UKWH00003B/1304

9 781300 308188